The
Connell Short Guide
to
Daphne du Maurier's

———————

Rebecca

———————

by
Theo Tait

Contents

Introduction

In April 1937, when she was 30 years old, Daphne du Maurier told her publisher Victor Gollancz that she wanted to write "rather a sinister tale about a woman who marries a widower... Psychological and rather macabre." A few months later, having given birth to her second daughter in London, she returned to Alexandria, where her husband Tommy Browning, a senior officer in the Grenadier Guards, had been posted – and began to write her fifth novel in the heat of the Egyptian summer. It was difficult. Du Maurier hated Egypt and its climate. Being somewhat shy and reclusive, she found it hard to perform her duties as the wife of the battalion commander – the round of cocktail parties and social functions. Her husband was ten years older than her, efficient and meticulous; Du Maurier felt that she had no talent for running a large house, even though that largely involved giving orders to the servants. She felt isolated and longed for England.

"I was homesick for Cornwall," she wrote later: her family had a holiday home near Fowey. In particular, she found herself thinking about Menabilly, a large, empty house hidden in the woods on an isolated headland. She had heard that the owner had been married first to a very beautiful woman, and had then married again, to a much younger one. There was a rumour that he had left the place empty because he found his first wife in the arms of her lover there. Various other influences played on her mind. She was jealous of her husband's one-time fiancée Jan Ricardo. According to her biographer Margaret Forster, "she was still haunted by the suspicion that Tommy had found the beautiful, dark-haired, glamorous Jan more attractive than herself"; her "feelings of inferiority in this respect, and of being intimidated, went straight into the character of the second Mrs de Winter". "Seeds began to drop," wrote du Maurier in *The Rebecca Notebook*. "A beautiful home... a first wife... jealousy... a wreck, perhaps at sea, near to the house..." She also remembered a tall, sinister-looking housekeeper whom she had seen at a large house she had visited as a child in Northamptonshire.

Du Maurier threw away a first draft of the novel, 15,000 words long, in Egypt, leaving her with little more than a title, *Rebecca*, and a few notes. "Very roughly," she wrote to Gollancz, "the book will be about the influence of a first wife on a second... she is dead before the book opens. Little by little I want to build up the character of the first wife in the mind of the second... until wife 2 is haunted day and night... a tragedy is looming very close and crash! bang! something happens..." But she was unable to think what this something might be. She and her husband returned to England in December, with only a quarter of the novel finished. The rest of it was written by the sea in Cornwall, and in Hampshire, where Browning was stationed.

By this point, du Maurier was already a successful author with four novels and two family biographies behind her. Her previous book, *Jamaica Inn* (1936), a tale of wreckers and smugglers in 19th century Cornwall, had been a great success. But her publishers could immediately see that *Rebecca* would be even bigger. Gollancz was delighted; her editor, Norman Collins, remarked: "The new Daphne du Maurier contains everything that the public could want."

Rebecca was published in 1938. It was immediately a great popular success, though the critical reaction was lukewarm. Reviewers mostly praised it, but in rather derogatory terms, noting its "popular appeal" and dismissing it as an "unashamed melodrama". *The Sunday Times* labeled *Rebecca* a "romance in the grand tradition". "Nothing in this is beyond the novelette," declared *The Times* - though its reviewer admitted that there was "an atmosphere of terror which... makes it easy to overlook... the weaknesses". "It would be absurd to make a fuss about *Rebecca*," wrote V.S. Pritchett, one of the period's leading critics in the *Christian Science Monitor*. "It will be here today and gone tomorrow like the rest of publicity's 'masterpieces'." Only *The Observer*'s Frank Swinnerton discerned something more, describing "the fearlessness with which Miss du Maurier works in material so strange" as "magnificent". The "sniggers of meticulous sophisticates", he felt, should be ignored. *Rebecca* sold in large numbers, with 60,000 copies quickly sold in Britain and America, and was made into an admired Alfred Hitchcock film in 1939.

It has continued to be popular ever since, if not prestigious. For instance, when F. Scott Fitzgerald wanted to disparage his former friend Ernest Hemingway's *For Whom the Bell Tolls* (1940), he described it as "a thoroughly superficial book which has all the profundity of *Rebecca*". Yet du Maurier's novel has never been out of print; today, 75 years after publication, it still sells thousands of copies around the world every month. It has been immensely influential on popular storytelling. Well-respected writers have provided a prequel and a sequel – respectively, Sally Beauman's *Rebecca's Tale* (2001) and Susan Hill's *Mrs De Winter* (1993) – while various other writers, from Stephen King to Antonia Fraser, have paid homage to it in their own works of fiction.

For decades *Rebecca*, along with the rest of du Maurier's work, was filed away as "romantic fiction", "gothic fiction" or "gothic romance", meaning that it did not qualify as proper "English literature". In recent years, however, du Maurier's reputation has risen – partly because gothic fiction and female writers have become a more respectable subject for academic and critical attention, and partly due to the three classic films that have been made of her stories, two by Alfred Hitchcock – *Rebecca* and *The Birds* (1963) - and one by Nicholas Roeg, *Don't Look Now* (1973). Today, writes the cultural critic Christopher Frayling, "her work looks increasingly rich and dark": atmospheric and straightforwardly entertaining, but also offering interesting perspectives on individual psychology, family, class and gender roles. *Rebecca* is generally regarded as du Maurier's masterpiece.

A summary of the plot

Chapter 1: The book begins, famously, with the nameless narrator describing her dream of returning to Manderley, a grand house near the coast in the west country, and finding it empty and neglected.

Chapter 2: The narrator and her husband, in refuge from painful events in the past, live in a small, spartan hotel somewhere in southern Europe – dreaming of England and of Manderley. The narrator remembers her first meeting with her husband, Maxim de Winter, when she was staying in a hotel in Monte Carlo, the paid companion of Mrs Van Hopper, a vulgar American.

Chapter 3: Mrs Van Hopper inveigles Maxim, an acquaintance, into a conversation. He is clearly embarrassed by Mrs Van Hopper, and makes jokes at her expense; later he writes to the narrator apologising for his rudeness.

Chapter 4: While her employer is ill, Maxim insists that the narrator should have lunch with him, and takes her for a drive; he is kind and attentive, though odd. Mrs Van Hopper explains that his first wife Rebecca died in an "appalling tragedy", drowning in a bay near Manderley.

Chapter 5: Maxim and the narrator continue to spend the mornings together; she hides her activities from Mrs Van Hopper. She falls in love with him, but thinks him indifferent. When she asks whether he spends time with her out of charity, he gets angry – but kisses her.

Chapter 6: Mrs Van Hopper plans to go to America. When the narrator tells Maxim, he responds by asking her, curtly, to marry him. She accepts, and Maxim tells Mrs Van Hopper – who tells him that she will never manage as "mistress of Manderley".

Chapter 7: They arrive at Manderley from London. As the narrator is introduced to the staff – especially the intimidating housekeeper, Mrs Danvers – she feels uneasy in her new role.

Chapter 8: As she tries to run the house, the narrator commits various minor blunders.

Chapter 9: Maxim's kind, bluff sister Beatrice and her husband Giles come to visit, along with the estate manager Frank Crawley.

Chapter 10: Maxim and the narrator walk down to the sea, and the dog leads her to a run-down cottage in a cove; Maxim is angry, revealing that he never goes to that "god-damned" place.

Chapter 11: The narrator receives various local dignitaries; she finds it all difficult, and thinks everyone is comparing her to Rebecca. Frank tries to reassure her, and also tells her that Rebecca died at night, having gone sailing on her own.

Chapter 12: The narrator breaks a china cupid, and hides it out of embarrassment. Mrs Danvers accuses a servant, Robert, of stealing it; the narrator has to tell everyone that it was her.

Chapter 13: While Maxim is away in London, the narrator discovers a dissolute character called Jack Favell paying a visit to the house.

Chapter 14: The narrator goes to Rebecca's bedroom and is surprised by Mrs Danvers there. Mrs Danvers has kept the room exactly as it was, and speaks about her great admiration for Rebecca.

Chapter 15: Beatrice takes the narrator to visit Maxim's grandmother in a nursing home. On their return, the narrator hears Maxim upbraiding Mrs Danvers furiously for allowing Jack Favell into the house.

Chapter 16: Maxim agrees to hold the traditional fancy dress ball at Manderley. On Mrs Danvers's advice, the narrator dresses up as an ancestor of Maxim's depicted in a painting. She keeps her decision a secret; when she comes down, Maxim is furious and orders her to change.

Chapter 17: Beatrice explains Maxim's fury:

Rebecca had worn exactly the same outfit at last year's ball, and Maxim has assumed that she is playing some trick on him. Beatrice begs her to put on an ordinary dress and come back down. The night is a terrible trial for her.

Chapter 18: The narrator wakes to find Maxim gone; she believes that Maxim has never loved her, and still loves Rebecca. She confronts Mrs Danvers in Rebecca's old bedroom. Mrs Danvers is unrepentant, and encourages her to jump from the window. Then a ship runs ashore in the bay.

Chapter 19: A diver is sent down to look at the ship, and finds Rebecca's boat there, with a body in it. Maxim reveals that the body is Rebecca's – even though he had identified a body washed up down the coast as hers – and that he, in fact, killed her.

Chapter 20: Maxim tells the narrator, at last, that he loves her: far from loving Rebecca, he hated her. She was an immoral and unfaithful "devil". He says that he shot Rebecca, after she had told him that she was pregnant with an illegitimate child, then took her out in her boat and sunk it.

Chapter 21: Colonel Julyan, the local magistrate, reveals that the boat has been raised, and Rebecca's body identified. There will need to be a new inquest, though Julyan appears satisfied that a simple mistake of identification has been made.

Chapter 22: The narrator and Maxim go to the local market town for the coroner's inquest. Tabb the boat builder reveals that the boat has been deliberately scuttled. The coroner asks Maxim for an explanation. The narrator faints.

Chapter 23: The coroner reaches a verdict of suicide. Jack Favell then arrives at Manderley, announcing that he knows it wasn't suicide. He reveals that he and Rebecca were lovers; and tries to blackmail Maxim. Maxim summons Colonel Julyan. Favell tells him that Maxim murdered Rebecca.

Chapter 24: Favell argues that Maxim killed Rebecca out of jealousy. Julyan asks for proof. Favell calls Ben, the "local half-wit" who is often down at the cove, as a witness; but Ben says he saw nothing. They discover that Rebecca had had a doctor's appointment the day that she died.

Chapter 25: They decide to visit the specialist, Dr Baker, now retired in Barnet. Mrs Danvers learns that Favell suspects Maxim of murder. Julyan also now seems to have his suspicions.

Chapter 26: Dr Baker, a women's specialist, reveals that Rebecca had indeed visited that day, under the name of Mrs Danvers, and was "seriously ill" – suffering from terminal cancer.

Chapter 27: Julyan promises to let it be known that Rebecca committed suicide, but suggests that the narrator take a short holiday abroad while the gossip dies down. Maxim phones Manderley, and discovers that Mrs Danvers has disappeared, shortly after receiving a long distance call – presumably from Favell. Worried, Maxim decides to return to Manderley. He and his wife drive back, and as they near Manderley they see that the house is on fire.

Models and precursors

Gothic romance

What do people mean when they refer to *Rebecca* as a Gothic romance? The academic Richard Kelly suggests that it has "most of the trappings" of the genre: "a mysterious, haunted mansion, violence, murder, a sinister villain, sexual passion, a spectacular fire, a brooding landscape..." The quintessential Gothic romance is Ann Radcliffe's *The Mysteries of Udolpho* (1794).

Nowadays remembered chiefly as the target of Jane Austen's Gothic satire, *Northanger Abbey* (1817), *The Mysteries of Udolpho* is set in 16th century Europe and tells the story of a young, orphaned French noblewoman who is imprisoned in Udolpho, a castle in Italy, by her aunt's husband – a scheming brigand who tries to force her to marry his friend. Eventually she escapes, and is reunited with her true love. The novel spawned a genre, which typically includes many of the following features: a persecuted heroine, usually an orphan; wild, remote landscapes and forests;

large, crumbling castles or mansions; psychological terror; a Byronic villain; a family secret or curse.

The form is descended from fairy-tale and medieval romance, but in Radcliffe's version of it the supernatural is always explained away: apparently ghostly events are revealed to have a rational explanation – usually an attempt by the villain to terrify and gain control over the woman and her property. Gothic romance was usually written by women, for women; it is sometimes called "the female Gothic", or "the feminine Gothic". Tania Modleski suggests that it provided "an outlet for women's fears about their husbands and fathers". Offering an exaggerated vision of the typical male-dominated family, it "spoke powerfully to the young girl struggling to maintain psychic autonomy" in a house where a remote but all-powerful father or husband "ruled over an utterly dependent wife".

During the course of the 19th century, Gothic romance was progressively domesticated, made more modern and realistic. Henry James pointed out that in the work of Mary Elizabeth Braddon – "novels of sensation" such as *Lady Audley's Secret* (1862) – the lurid terrors of Radcliffe's stories were transposed to the contemporary "country house or the London lodgings". Much of du Maurier's work was in this tradition. *Jamaica Inn*, like *The Mysteries of Udolpho*, features a young orphaned heroine who has to live with her aunt and menacing uncle in a remote location. *Rebecca*, which also features an orphan, takes many Gothic features and sets them in a modern environment; its tense country house atmosphere, and its twisty plot, probably owe something to *Lady Audley's Secret*. It may also have been influenced by Elizabeth von Arnim's *Vera* (1921), in which a naive, recently orphaned young woman is swept up into a marriage with a controlling, bullying widower. Again, the first wife has died in mysterious circumstances, and again his mansion is pervaded by the presence of his dead wife, Vera.

Jane Eyre

The novelist Angela Carter claimed that *Rebecca* "shamelessly reduplicated" the plot of Charlotte Brontë's *Jane Eyre* (1847); many critics before and since have claimed that du Maurier's novel is indebted to Brontë's. There are many clear parallels, here listed by Patsy Stoneman:

> The young heroine is like Jane Eyre in being an orphan, humble, shy and diffident, and her occupation, as companion to a rich lady, is similar in status to that of a Victorian governess [Jane's job]. Max de Winter is like Rochester [Brontë's hero] in being rich and independent, the owner of a country house, and in having an unhappy secret

which makes him moody and inward looking. The two secrets are similar (first wives who were brilliant but immoral) and both have attempted to rid themselves of their wives by illegal means. In both cases, the country house becomes oppressive to its owner because of its association with the mad, bad wife. In spite of being haunted and oppressed, however, by the houses which contain evidence of disastrous first marriages, both Rochester and Max de Winter try to establish new, young wives in the same houses and under the same domestic rules.

In addition, in both cases the men's country houses burn to the ground in spectacular fires. (In an earlier draft of *Rebecca*, Maxim was badly injured in the fire, like Rochester.) Happy-ish endings are achieved, but at a great price. More specifically, the opening dream of Manderley – dreams play an important role in both novels – is suggested by Jane's nightmare in which Thornfield Hall, Rochester's home, has become "a dreary ruin".

Both books reimagine the Gothic trope of the family secret in a similar way. Maria Tatar has suggested that both are variants of the folktale of Bluebeard, in which a young woman marries a rich stranger whose castle contains a forbidden room; the young woman enters the room, and discovers the murdered bodies of his previous wives. In *Jane Eyre* and *Rebecca*, however, the previous wife is a powerful and predatory figure rather than a victim. Jane's questions in Chapter 20 of *Jane Eyre* could apply to both books:

> What crime was this, that lived incarnate in this sequestered mansion, and could neither be expelled nor subdued by the owner? What mystery, that broke out now in fire and now in blood, at the deadest hours of night? What creature was it, that, masked in an ordinary woman's face and shape, uttered the voice, now of a mocking demon, and anon of a carrion-seeking bird of prey?

There are, on the other hand, important differences between the two novels. *Jane Eyre* is a deeply, explicitly Christian novel; *Rebecca* is arguably amoral by Christian standards. *Rebecca* is a crime story; *Jane Eyre* is structured more like a parable, a pilgrim's progress. *Rebecca* is anxiously obsessed with social class; *Jane Eyre* – though not unimpressed by its trappings – regards class as a worldly obstacle to be overcome. Jane Eyre is very brave and unconventional; the narrator of *Rebecca* is timid and wants to fit in. It is probably fairer to regard *Rebecca* as a rewriting of *Jane Eyre*, rather than a reduplication, just as *Jane Eyre* is a rewriting of earlier Gothic novels (and Angela Carter's own story *The Bloody Chamber* is a rewriting of the tale of Bluebeard). Indeed, between them, *Jane Eyre* and *Rebecca* have formed their own mini-tradition. According to Joanna Russ, the Mills & Boon-style genre of "Modern Gothic", a cross-breed of the two, follows this formula:

> To a large, lonely, brooding House (always named) comes a Heroine who is young, orphaned, unloved and lonely. She is shy and inexperienced. She is attractive, sometimes even beautiful, but she does not know it. The House is set in exotic, vivid and/or exotic Country. [The Heroine] forms a personal or professional connection with an older man, a dark, magnetic, powerful, brooding, sardonic Super-Male, who treats her brusquely, derogates, scolds her and otherwise shows anger or contempt for her... In the emotionally tangled and darkly mysterious "family" set up in our House are hints of the presence of the Other Woman who is at the same time her double and her opposite – very often she is the Super-Male's present wife or first dead wife. The Other Woman is (or was) beautiful, worldly, glamorous, immoral, flirtatious, irresponsible and openly sexual. [The Heroine] gradually becomes aware that somewhere in the tangle of oppressive family secrets going on in the House exists a Buried Ominous Secret, always connected with the Other Woman and the Super-Male...

Plot

Rebecca is a story about the past and its influence on the present, and it moves between the two. It begins at the end – with the house destroyed, and Maxim and the narrator living abroad – then loops back to the beginning. Broadly speaking, the novel is made up of two plots, one about the present and one about the past. One is a romance story – a modern variant of the Cinderella plot, similar perhaps to the novels of du Maurier's contemporary Barbara Cartland, in which, against all the odds, a penniless orphan – "the raw ex-schoolgirl, red-elbowed and lanky-haired" (3)* – marries a great nobleman, "the man who owns Manderley" (2). After receiving Maxim's proposal, the narrator thinks: "Romantic. That was what people would say. It was all very sudden and romantic" (6). Yet their courtship is not actually very romantic, or at least not straightforwardly so; Maxim doesn't court her in any obvious way. She falls in love with him, but he is distant and cold, and she thinks he regards her as a daughter or a sister. He then makes his famously charmless wedding proposal: "No, I'm asking you to marry me, you little fool" (6). And, as Alison Light points out, whereas most romances end with the marriage of the lovers, "the girl's romance and whirlwind marriage... only

*Numbers in brackets refer to the chapters from which the quotations are taken.

occupy about one eighth of *Rebecca*". Thereafter, it becomes a "thriller which goes behind the scenes of the romance drama", exposing the Prince Charming character as a criminal.

In fact, the book could be divided into three quite distinct sections, each with a distinct mood. Screenwriters sometimes say that a classic story will divide up into three acts, each of which builds up to a climactic twist or reversal that takes the action into a different direction. This is certainly true of *Rebecca*. There is the courtship section, set in Monte Carlo, which builds up to the revelation that Maxim wants to marry the narrator. Then there is the Manderley section, building up to revelation that Maxim, far from being still in love with his ex-wife, hated her so much that he killed her. Finally, there is the investigation, which builds up to the revelation that Rebecca was dying of cancer, and so had a motive for suicide, putting Maxim in the clear. If the first part is a kind of romance, the second part is a Gothic mystery: brooding and atmospheric, very like a ghost story, except that, as in Ann Radcliffe's novels, the supernatural is (mostly) explained. Think how many of the tropes of the ghost story du Maurier deploys: the pale face at the window; the eerie, unused section of the house; the deserted cottage; the murdered body, hastily disposed of, which will "come back and haunt the living", in Mrs Danvers's words (14). The final act is very different again:

some have compared it to an Agatha Christie novel, or a police procedural.

But throughout, the organising principle of the plot is suspense, the gradual explanation of a mystery or series of mysteries, the exposure of "unknown things that lay beneath" (19). In her notebooks, du Maurier wrote that she wanted to "build it up little by little". Her editor Sheila Hodges added that it was "important to her that each chapter should end on as tantalising a note as possible, so that the reader would be compelled to carry on with the next one". In *Rebecca*, the reader is given a steady drip of revelations about the past, often at the end of a chapter. The final line of Chapter 2, just after we have been introduced to Maxim, is: "They say he can't get over his wife's death." At the end of Chapter 4, Mrs Van Hopper reveals that it was an "an appalling tragedy": "She was drowned you know, in the bay near Manderley..." "Little by little shall I understand," says the narrator later on in the book: "all that has happened will tumble into place like pieces of jig-saw puzzle" (20). The novel provides a steady drip of partial disclosures that gradually reveal the truth about Maxim and Rebecca's life together.

For instance, when the narrator walks to Rebecca's cottage by the cove, a furious Maxim says that he never goes near "the bloody place". Echoing Bluebeard, he warns her away from the scene of the crime: "If you had my memories you would not go there either" (10). Meanwhile, beneath the praise for Rebecca a sinister undercurrent gradually becomes discernible: we learn that Ben was terrified of Rebecca, while Frank Crawley hints that while she was witty, charming and the "most beautiful creature I ever saw in my life", she also lacked kindness, sincerity and, most importantly, "modesty" (11). The narrator doesn't quite know what he means, but her suspicions are increased after her cousin Jack Favell, "sensuous", "attractive" and "disreputable", arrives at the house and refers suggestively to his close friendship with his cousin (13). The plot thickens when Mrs Danvers reveals that Rebecca met men in London who "made love to her", presumably in the 1930s sense of the phrase (18).

Then, in Chapter 19, all the jig-saw pieces tumble into place: Rebecca's body is still in her boat; she was repeatedly unfaithful to Maxim; and – at the end of the chapter, of course – is the revelation that he killed her. Even then, there are a number of further twists to come, each usually heralded by an end-of-chapter flourish: a telephone ringing suddenly; the narrator fainting in the courtroom; and, last of all, the discovery Manderley has been set on fire.

Style

When du Maurier first sent *Rebecca* to Gollancz, she was worried that he would think it "overdone". And in the opinion of many critics, it is. John Sutherland calls her prose "excessively and lushly descriptive"; Sally Beauman calls the first chapter "slightly scented and over-written, that of a schoolgirl, trying to speak poetically, and struggling to impress".

Du Maurier's style is certainly fairly ripe. She specialises in lilting, rhythmic sentences. Many of these have, however, been much admired . The first line of *Rebecca*, for instance–"Last night I dreamt I went to Manderley again" – is one of the most famous in 20th century English fiction, and has often been praised for establishing the voice and the dream-like atmosphere of the story in one stroke. It is an iambic hexameter – a line of six feet, each consisting of two syllables, the first unstressed and the second stressed. The last line – "And the ashes blew towards us with the salt wind from the sea" – is equally rhythmic, though consisting (more or less) of a string of anapests: two short syllables followed by a long one. Her sentences often involve piling detail upon detail, using multiple clauses of the same kind. On the drive to Manderley, for instance, "there was no

Opposite: Daphne du Maurier in 1931, the year her first novel, The Loving Spirit, *was published*

house, no field, no broad and friendly garden, nothing but the silence and deep woods" (7). Or: "The fog filled the open window, damp and clammy, it stung to my eyes, it clung to my nostrils" (18). Or: "I know how many grouse are killed, how many partridge, how many head of deer. I know where trout are rising, and where the salmon leap" (1).

Yet the language of *Rebecca* is also relatively simple and easy to absorb; du Maurier aimed at "simplicity of style". There are few complex or obscure words. The only words that are difficult are the ones that are no longer used: words like "maroon", meaning a warning rocket (21), and trade names like Taxol, a cure for indigestion (5), the elastic fabric Stockinette (7), or Banting, a diet regime named after its inventor (25).

Du Maurier is arguably a writer of limited and erratic stylistic resources. Sheila Hodges, her editor, has revealed that a lot of work was required to get her novels into a publishable form. Her spelling and punctuation were poor; "her writing tended to be tautological, and sometimes considerable cutting was necessary". She certainly repeats herself a great deal. "It made me want to scream. I wanted to run out of the room and scream and scream" (24). She often repeats the same verbal formula again and again, within a few pages:

He began to laugh. He stood there laughing. I could

not bear it, it made me frightened, ill. (20)

She began to laugh. She went on laughing. I thought she would never stop. (20)

And Favell began to laugh, the laugh of a drunkard, high-pitched, forced, and foolish, and all the while twisting Rebecca's note between his fingers. (23)

He looked round at each one of us and began to laugh. (25)

There is also a kind of endemic exaggeration in her writing. To take a minor example, we are told that when she is driving, Beatrice "kept her foot permanently on the accelerator, and took every corner at an acute angle". (An acute angle means one of smaller than 90 degrees, which sounds dangerous.) Equally, it hardly seems believable when the narrator claims to know "the name of every owner of every British moor, yes – and their tenants too... Even the names of those who walk hound puppies are familiar to me" (2). Du Maurier's use of language is sometimes florid without being expressive: she deploys romantic cliché s such as "the fury was spent" (24). Her lines can also be florid and garbled at the same time: "Poor whims of fancy, tender and un-harsh" (1).

And yet both the excessiveness and the repetition in her prose can be powerful.

Responding to the criticism that one of her earlier books was overwritten, du Maurier responded: "Yes, of course it's overwritten, but then in a sense that was deliberately done. I wanted to ooze blood and diarrhoea all over it..." That in itself sounds like an exaggeration, but there is an element of truth to it. Consider the moment when the narrator arrives at Manderley for the first time, and finds that on either side of her there is "a wall of colour, blood-red, reaching far above our heads":

We were amongst the rhododendrons. There was something bewildering, even shocking, about the suddenness of their discovery... They startled me with their crimson faces, massed one upon the other in incredible profusion, showing no leaf, no twig, nothing but the slaughterous red, luscious and fantastic, unlike any rhododendron plant I had seen before. (7)

Her insistent, rhythmic prose, piling up detail and visceral imagery, is excessive, but it creates a powerful atmosphere. *Rebecca* is a book about obsession, and it obsessively reiterates its themes. It repeats various phrases and words again and again, like a refrain: the idea of "going back"; the phrase "I could imagine"; the word "Manderley"; and of course the name "Rebecca":

He did not belong to me at all, he belonged to

Rebecca. He still thought about Rebecca. He would never love me because of Rebecca... Rebecca, always Rebecca. Wherever I walked in Manderley, wherever I sat, even in my thoughts and in my dreams, I met Rebecca. (18)

All this, of course, is a verbal form of "going back": obsessively returning to the same subjects.

Atmosphere

In her notebook for *Rebecca*, du Maurier wrote a list of her guiding principles for the novel. First came "atmosphere". Du Maurier is often praised for her ability to create atmosphere, to evoke the essence of particular places. This is partly a question of the setting (the main part of the story takes place in Cornwall, though the county, as opposed to the "west country", is never actually mentioned in the book). Stories set in wild, remote areas had been attractive to the largely urban book-buying audience since the early 19th century; the idea of a beautiful house ringed by thick woods is a feature of fairytales such as Sleeping Beauty, and of Gothic novels. But the atmosphere of *Rebecca* is also to a large extent a result of how closely the details of the external world, especially the natural world, correlate with the psychological states of the characters – particularly the narrator's.

For instance, when the second Mrs de Winter is living at Manderley, uneasy about her husband and her marriage, she is haunted by the sound of the sea:

A dull, persistent sound that never ceased... I began to understand why some people could not bear the clamour of the sea. It has a mournful harping note sometimes, and the very persistence of it, that eternal roll and thunder and hiss, plays a jagged tune upon the nerves. (11)

Later, when Mrs Danvers is trying to persuade the desperate narrator to throw herself out of the window, fog covers the terrace, evoking her isolation and confusion:

The fog came thicker than before and the terrace was hidden from me. I could not see the flower tubs any more, nor the smooth paved stones. There was the nothing but the white mist about me, smelling of sea-weed dank and chill. (18)

Later still, when Rebecca's boat has been raised and her body identified, and the de Winters are waiting anxiously for next development, the weather reflects her mood of tense expectation:

The weather had not broken yet. It was still hot, oppressive. The air was full of thunder, and there

was rain behind the white dull sky, but it did not fall.
(22)

At the inquest, when Tabb the boatbuilder declares that someone had scuttled the boat, the narrator suddenly finds it "hot, much too hot" (22). In the final act, when the worst has happened and Maxim has been accused of murder, the weather breaks and finally the rain falls.

Most novels contain significant symbols, physical details of the story that also have a larger representative role; John Ruskin coined the phrase "the pathetic fallacy" to describe the widespread artistic tendency to attribute human emotion to aspects of nature. But du Maurier takes this technique so far that her method here could be called Expressionist. Expressionism was an artistic movement during the early 20th century, which aimed to represent the world in a way that expressed subjective, and often violent, human emotion – distorting it to express moods and feelings, rather than aiming to offer an objective picture of the world. So, when the narrator and Maxim have to leave Manderley for the last time, their bedroom reflects their feelings:

> *The dressing-table was bare without my brushes...*
> *The beds where we had slept had a terrible*
> *emptiness about them... The wardrobe doors gaped*
> *open. (26)*

Similarly, the rhododendrons discussed in the previous chapter are loaded with all sorts of ominous significance – intimations of murder ("blood-red", "slaughterous") and an almost sexual excess ("luscious and fantastic").

After the inquest, when the narrator fears that her husband may be charged with murder – and possibly hanged – the hydrangeas on the drive are "sombre" and "funereal... like the wreaths, stiff and artificial, that you see beneath glass cases in a foreign churchyard" (23). This Expressionist tendency is, in part, why du Maurier's books film so well: they offer compelling visual correlatives for their characters' emotional states. Her tendency to overwrite, which has been deplored, and her gift for atmosphere, which has been admired, are arguably two sides of the same coin.

Themes

Jealousy

According to Daphne du Maurier's son Kit Browning, the author regarded *Rebecca* as primarily a "study in jealousy". From very early on in the story – as soon as she begins to fall in love with Maxim – the narrator is assailed by descriptions of Rebecca's beauty and accomplishments. "I never saw her," says Mrs Van Hopper, "but I believe she was very lovely. Exquisitely turned out, and brilliant in every way" (5). Already, the narrator's thoughts are turned, somewhat obsessively, towards Maxim's first wife: "I was following a phantom in my mind, whose shadowy form had taken shape at last." To a shy, inexperienced young woman, even the dedication in the book of poetry that Maxim lends her carries intimations of Rebecca's superiority: "That bold, slanting hand, stabbing the white paper, the symbol of herself, so certain, so assured." Rebecca called him Max; she is asked to call him Maxim – the name, she thinks for "Grandmothers and people like myself, quiet and dull and youthful, who did not matter". She immediately perceives herself to be in a struggle with Rebecca, one with undertones of violence: after Maxim's marriage proposal, she not only tears out the inscription from the book, but burns the pieces (6).

From the arrival in Manderley, almost every incident reflects the narrator's sense of inferiority. Where Rebecca ran the house like clockwork, she is clueless and commits a series of faux pas. Where Rebecca lived in the grand west wing, the narrator is given the less impressive east wing "a second-rate room, as it were, for a second-rate person" (7). Mrs Danvers loved Rebecca; she despises the narrator. Everyone seems, certainly in the narrator's mind, to compare her unfavourably to her predecessor. The narrator imagines visitors saying: "My dear, what a dull girl... She's so different from Rebecca" (11).

Frank says that Rebecca was "the most beautiful creature I ever saw in my life". Rebecca always charmed Maxim's grandmother, who rejects the narrator as "a child" whom she doesn't know (15). Where Rebecca was brave, full of life, and passionate, the narrator is "a wooden thing in Maxim's arms" (20). In Chapter 18, the narrator summarises all of her fears and jealousies. Maxim doesn't love her; he loves Rebecca. The servants obey her orders. The house is decorated to her designs. "Rebecca was still mistress of Manderley. Rebecca was still Mrs de Winter. I had no business here at all. I had come blundering like a poor fool on ground that was preserved." Following the climactic revelation, however, the main cause of the jealousy is proved to be groundless: "You thought I loved Rebecca?" says Maxim. "You thought I killed her, loving her. I hated her, I tell you. Our marriage was a farce from the very first" (20). This makes the narrator "free of her forever" (21).

Dreams and day-dreaming

Rebecca begins with a dream of ruin and loss, of "the things we have tried to forget and put behind us" (2). And it ends with the second Mrs de Winter having a series of dreams in the car before they arrive at Manderley to find it burned down. One of these reprises the opening dream, of Manderley as a ruin; in the final one, she finds herself writing in Rebecca's handwriting, and seeing a "very pale, very lovely face, framed in a cloud of dark hair" – Rebecca's – staring back at her from the mirror (27). Earlier, she dreams that she is walking just behind Max in the woods "and could not keep up with him" (15).

The book is also filled with endless day-dreams. The phrase "I could imagine" is a constant refrain, along with "I pictured", "I wondered", "I began to think". There are long sequences in which, for instance, the narrator imagines being taken back to Manderley as Mrs de Winter, or imagines the ball; or, while at the ball, imagines people's comments afterwards. Her imagination is constantly running away with her: she imagines Maxim dead; she imagines Maxim down at the crypt, burying Rebecca's body; she frequently imagines the spirit of Rebecca haunting the house.

Rebecca is a dream-like book, and one in which life often takes on the quality of a dream. The narrator remembers the ball the following day "like an old forgotten nightmare" (21), and indeed the descriptions of the ball make it sound like one:

> *The background was hazy, a sea of dim faces none of whom I knew, and there was the slow drone of the band harping out a waltz that never finished, that went on and on. The same couples swung by in rotation, with the same fixed smiles, and to me, standing with Maxim at the bottom of the stairs to welcome the late-comers, these dancing couples seemed like marionettes twisting and turning on a piece of string, held by some invisible hand.* (17)

Du Maurier's grandfather, the novelist George du Maurier, invented in one of his early novels the concept of "dreaming true", a method whereby everything that the dreamer desires comes to him. It was an idea that fascinated Daphne. The dream-like atmosphere of *Rebecca* gives a sense of unconscious desires, and particularly fears, running close to the surface of normal life. The general tenor of the dreams and daydreams is uneasy, eerie and morbid: death, loss and ruin are recurring themes, as are a sense of inferiority and of being out of place. All of these focus, of course, on Rebecca: "Wherever I walked in Manderley, wherever I sat, even in my thoughts and in my dreams, I met Rebecca" (18).

The past and "going back"

The novel is phrased as a memory, as a flashback beginning in Chapter 2. In Chapter 1 the narrator dreams of Manderley, which is simultaneously sinister and filled with tender recollections (of tea in the library and of a beloved dog). The past, good and bad, is irrecoverable. Chapter 2 begins with the words: "We can never go back, that much is certain. The past is still too close to us."

Throughout the book, two versions of the past jostle against each other: nostalgia for things that were loved and are now lost; and the de Winters' attempt to put behind them the things they wish to forget. For instance, after experiencing a moment of great happiness in Maxim's car near Monte Carlo, the narrator wishes that there was an invention "that bottled memory, like scent. And it never faded, and it never got stale" (5). By contrast, Maxim wants to forget the past, he tells her shortly afterwards:

"All memories are bitter, and I prefer to forget them. Something happened a year ago that altered my whole life, and I want to forget every phase in my existence up to that time."

The idea of the past, and of going back to it, or bringing it back, is a regular refrain in the book. "I wanted to go back again, to recapture the moment that had gone," says the narrator of the time in the car (5). "I knew I should never go back," she says, as she describes packing up Mrs Van Hopper's suite (6). Frank tells the second Mrs de Winter to forget Rebecca: "We none of us want to bring back the past. Maxim least of all" (12). Visiting Rebecca's room is "like seeing back into Time" (14). The narrator becomes convinced that the past, in the form of Rebecca's ghostly presence, "might come back into the room" (8).

She feels like a guest waiting for "the return of the hostess" (12). And indeed the hostess does return, in her rediscovered boat, which has the "queer prophetic name" *Je Reviens*, or "I will come back" (21). Captain Searle, who is in charge of the salvage operation that finds Rebecca's boat says: "It's hard on him and hard on you that we can't let the past lie quiet" (19). Upon discovering Maxim's secret, the narrator declares: "The past can't hurt us if we are together" (23). The past, of course, does hurt them. They are eventually made "free" of the past, but the second Mrs de Winter feels that they "have paid for freedom" (2).

Class

"You will have your work cut out as mistress of Manderley," Mrs Van Hopper tells the narrator after learning that the latter is to marry Maxim. "To be perfectly frank, my dear, I simply can't see you doing it... You haven't the experience... you don't know that milieu" (6).

As we have seen, *Rebecca* is a study in jealousy and feelings of inferiority. Many of these feelings, in the narrator's case, are related to class. After Maxim's proposal she tells him that she's not the "sort of person" he ought to marry: "I don't belong to your sort of world for one thing" (6). Indeed she interprets his initial proposal as a job offer: "Do you want me to be a secretary or something?" And Maxim rather tactlessly jokes that "instead of being companion to Mrs Van Hopper you become mine, and your duties will be almost exactly the same".

Earlier, she has fantasised about being a sort of feudal underling, living in a "lodge" on the grounds, visited occasionally by Maxim, the lord. After the marriage, the narrator finds herself struggling with the duties expected of a woman of her social standing: ordering the servants around; chatting with the local dignitaries; managing the "monstrous silver-tea pot and kettle" at tea-time. While the narrator feels "badly bred" (20), Rebecca had "breeding" as well as charm and beauty (16 & 20). Likewise, when Maxim has been cleared and the narrator is sure of his love, her confidence expresses itself in class terms:

> *It was going to be very different in the future. I was not going to be nervous and shy with the servants any more. With Mrs Danvers gone I should learn bit by bit to control the house. I would go and interview the cook in the kitchen. They would like me, respect me. (27)*

Class permeates many aspects of the story. There is no doubt that much of Maxim's mystique emanates from his lands and status. Similarly, some of the horror he feels towards his first wife is to do with the threat she poses to his social standing. He can just about tolerate her affair with Jack Favell, but fears that she "might get hold of one of the workmen on the estate, someone from Kerrith, anyone... And then the bomb would have to fall. The gossip, the publicity I feared" (20). The final straw is the news that she is apparently about to give birth to an illegitimate child, who would inherit his name and position. Even the narrator's description of the overgrown plants on the drive to Manderley in the opening dream are tinged with class awareness: the tall rhododendrons had "entered into alien marriage with a host of nameless shrubs, poor, bastard things that clung about their roots as though conscious of their spurious origin" (1).

Alison Light suggests that *Rebecca* is a nostalgic lament for the decline of the aristocracy:

the decline of the aristocracy. It's a lingering farewell to the world of Monte Carlo and of paid companions, to splendid breakfasts and devoted servants, the ease and arrogance of life in a stately home like Manderley.

This is partially true. It was written at a time when the great stately homes of Britain were dying out, and much space is devoted to the joys of gracious living: before leaving it forever, the narrator lovingly contemplates "the peace of Manderley", its lawns and elegant rooms, tended by gardeners, maids, and butlers (20).* On the other hand, *Rebecca* has as its heroine a penniless middle-class woman, and as its anti-heroine an arrogant, high-handed upper-class one. When Jack Favell complains to the magistrate Colonel Julyan that the investigation is a stitch-up, we know that he is at least partly right:

> *"You're going to back de Winter. You won't let him down because you've dined with him, and he's dined with you. He's a big name down here. He's the owner of Manderley. You poor bloody little snob." (24)*

The novel's attitude towards class is ambiguously positioned, between admiration and criticism.

* *It is worth noting that word "peace": Rebecca was written in 1937 and 1938, when war seemed increasingly likely.*

FIVE FACTS
ABOUT *REBECCA*

1.
Neville Chamberlain is reputed to have been reading *Rebecca* when he flew to Munich to meet Hitler in 1938.

2.
America's Motion Picture Production Code did not allow criminals to get away with their crimes; this is why Rebecca's death in Hitchcock's film version is an accident, not a murder. The office enforcing the code also demanded that some "quite inescapable inferences of sex perversion" in the relationship between Rebecca and Mrs Danvers be removed.

3.
Du Maurier suggested that the novel was set "in the mid-twenties". One of the few bits of internal evidence that precisely date the book is the narrator's reference to "maroons" sounding in the streets of London when she was "very small": these were rockets used as a warning that German bombers were approaching during World War One. This would suggest that the narrator was born around the same time as the author, 1907, and that the action of the novel takes place in the mid to late 1920s.

4.
Maxim was initially called Henry, but du Maurier changed it because she thought the name was "too dull".

5.
In 1940, when *Rebecca* was translated into Portuguese, it was claimed that du Maurier had stolen the plot from Carolina Nabuco's *A Sucessora* (1934). She was also sued, unsuccessfully, in 1947, on the grounds that she had plagiarised Edwina L. Macdonald's *Blind Windows* (1927).

The main characters

The narrator

Even though the reader spends the entire novel in the narrator's company, there is a lot we don't find out about her. Like most gothic heroines, she is an orphan. Her family are "dead", she tells Maxim (4), but the story is passed on only vaguely and briefly: her father died suddenly of pneumonia, and her mother followed soon afterwards, leaving her with no home or money. Famously, we never even learn her name. Maxim tells her that she has "a lovely and unusual name", to which she responds: "My father was a lovely and unusual person."

Du Maurier wrote in *The Rebecca Notebook* that she could not think of a name, and that not using one "became a challenge in technique, the easier because I was writing in the first person". Some critics have seen this decision from a feminist perspective: the narrator has no name of her own; her father gives her one name, and her husband the other. In the story, suggests Alison Light, she "searches to find a secure social identity (a name) as Maxim's wife".

John Sutherland writes that the narrator's "complete absence of history, past life or identity creates a striking vacuousness at the heart of the novel" – a vacuum which, he argues, is filled by

Rebecca: "In life the nameless one is less alive than dead Rebecca." Certainly, the narrator portrays herself as a less than a fully-fledged person. She calls herself "a lay-figure" – an artist's mannequin (16), "a dummy" (17), "a wooden thing in Maxim's arms" (20). As we have seen above, she is anxious and jealous of her predecessor, who seems to have had all the beauty, charm, experience and breeding that she lacks – the polar opposite of "the raw ex-schoolgirl, red-elbowed and lanky-haired" (2). In Chapters 7 to 18, every beat of the plot concerns her inferiority, her failure to perform effectively as Maxim's wife. The philosopher and critic Slavoj Zizek suggests that in her books, du Maurier again and again stages dramas of "feminine masochism". This section of the book gives full rein to this tendency. The narrator says that she loved him "in a sick, hurt, desperate way, like a child or a dog" (18).

However, she undergoes a transformation in the course of the book. Early on, she tends to be referred to as a girl or a child; Maxim suggests three times that she go to the ball as Alice in Wonderland – a young, curious girl. As mentioned above, he says pointedly that "there is a certain kind of knowledge I prefer you not to have" (16). She changes when she discovers that Maxim killed Rebecca – a mutation which is somewhat disquieting. She has no moral qualms following the discovery that her husband is a murderer, of both a woman and her unborn child: "there was no horror in my heart", she says (20).

Rather, she seems delighted: the phrase "He did not love Rebecca, he did not love Rebecca" repeats itself in her head (21). She becomes, legally, an accessory after the fact. Having exorcised the spirit of the first Mrs de Winter ("She would never haunt me again"), she reaches maturity, of an explicitly amoral sort:

> *I was not young any more. I was not shy. I was not afraid. I would fight for Maxim. I would lie and perjure and swear, I would blaspheme and pray. Rebecca had not won. Rebecca had lost. (21)*

Ultimately, though, her triumph is not a happy one. Sally Beauman suggests that her reward is to be "subsumed by her husband": following him into "hellish exile", she "becomes again what she was when she first met him – the paid companion to a petty tyrant". Perhaps this is an exaggeration, but her fate is certainly ambiguous.

Maxim

Maxim de Winter is positioned in *Rebecca* as the romantic hero, as the object of admiration, love and yearning – but very ambivalently so. On his first appearance, he is intimated to be firstly, handsome, rich and socially desirable, in the style of romantic heroes from Jane Austen to Jilly

Cooper; and secondly, clearly sinister. The narrator says that "his face was arresting, sensitive, medieval in some strange inexplicable way" (3). He reminds her of a portrait of a "Gentleman Unknown", evoking "a past of narrow stairways and dim dungeons, a past of whispers in the dark, of shimmering rapier blades, of silent, exquisite courtesy". It has been noted that the word maxim has two meanings. One is the dictionary definition: "a short, pithy statement expressing a general truth or rule of conduct." ("It was as if he had set himself a standard of behaviour," the narrator says of his good manners in listening to Mrs Van Hopper's inane prattle [3].) But a Maxim is also a British machine gun of the period, associated with slaughter in the colonies and the trenches. The name de Winter, furthermore, hints at something sterile and cold.

Maxim is in some respects a model gentleman. "He'd give the coat off his back for any of his own people, I know that," says the coastguard. "I wish there were more people like him in the county" (19). He is also capable of impeccable manners. But he is often impolite. In the lift, he looks down at the narrator and Mrs Van Hopper, "mocking, faintly, sardonic, a ghost of a smile on his lips" (5). From the off, Maxim intersperses episodes of kind attention towards the narrator with outbursts of anger and rudeness. His courtship is abrupt and sometimes unpleasant. "'To hell with this,' he said suddenly, as though angry, as though bored, and put his arm around my shoulder..." (5). His marriage proposal is rude: "No, I'm asking you to marry me, you little fool" (6). This is followed by an insult: "You are almost as ignorant as Mrs Van Hopper, and just as unintelligent." Maxim then suggests that he thought she loved him – while making no declaration of his own feelings, but sniffing that if she did not, it would have been "a fine blow to my conceit".

All this is perhaps standard for a romantic hero; they are often – like Mr Rochester – brusque, masterful and unattainable, as well as mentally turbulent. (The narrator fears, at the top of the cliff with him, that he is "not normal, not altogether sane" [4].) However, Maxim carries on being cold and unpleasant well into their marriage. There are suggestions that the marriage has, in the romantic and sexual sense, "failed": "The bed beside me looked stark and cold" (17). Note also the continued references to the possibility of the narrator being pregnant, while she is not. Again the connotations are sinister: at the ball, his eyes look beyond the narrator, "cold, expressionless, to some place of pain and torture I could not enter, to some private, inward hell I could not share" (17) – another echo, perhaps, of the Bluebeard theme.

These echoes are far from accidental: Maxim is, of course, a murderer. This was very shocking for a book of its time: so shocking that Hitchcock had to modify the story in his version, and make the death an accident. *Rebecca* asks us to become complicit with Maxim de Winter. And by and large, it succeeds: most readers want him to get away with murder. Some critics have suggested that Maxim's account of Rebecca's death – disturbing though it is – is not to be believed. John Sutherland points out that we know from the court scenes that he is "a liar on oath: a proven perjurer". Maxim claims that he took a loaded gun to Rebecca's cottage in order to "frighten the fellow, frighten them both" (20) – i.e. Rebecca and Favell – and that he was goaded into using it.

This is not a story that a jury would necessarily believe, particularly since we know that he has an explosive temper; and why would he bring a loaded gun just to frighten someone? Sutherland also notes, "as a passing point of interest, that Maxim has clearly shot people before": "I had forgotten," Maxim tells the narrator, "that when you shot a person there was so much blood" (20). Sutherland suggests that he probably served in the First World War; and notes the calm murderousness of his description: "I fired at her heart." Later, Maxim hits Favell in a rage; the narrator finds "something degrading" in this: "I wished I had not known" (24). How much else about him is she concealing from herself?

Rebecca

Just as Maxim is the hero, Rebecca is clearly the villainess of the story. On the face of it, the novel's ultimate judgment on her is Maxim's:

"She was vicious, damnable, rotten through and through... Rebecca was incapable of love, of tenderness, of decency." (20)

She is compared to "the devil", and, like some force of ancient evil, she is shot and sunk to the bottom of the sea, and even then returns to wreak havoc. Yet her position is just as ambiguous as Maxim's.

The book to some extent celebrates her (after all, it is named after her). If she was so awful, du Maurier's son Kit asked in an interview, "why is it that everybody else thought the sun shone out of her arse"? There's "never a bad word about Rebecca" in the book, he suggests, "except from Max". This is not quite right: Frank, Beatrice and Ben all hint at her bad behaviour, and even Mrs Danvers confirms that she was unfaithful to her husband. But it's true that most people are very impressed by her, from Maxim's grandmother, to the staff, and the doctor who admires the courage with which she received news of a terminal disease: "She stood it very well. She did not flinch" (26). And Maxim, as noted above, is a known liar. Aspects of his story do seem hard to credit: would she really, as suggested, have "started on" Giles sexually (20)? Giles is an amiable buffoon, and Rebecca is, according to Frank, "the most beautiful woman I ever saw in my life" (11). Indeed Antonia Fraser wrote a short piece of fiction seeing the events of the novel from Rebecca's point of view: Maxim is cast as a cruel monster suffering from some unspecified form of perversion, and Rebecca the wronged wife.

The book does not really support this: the most obvious interpretation is that Rebecca is devious and covers up her true personality. "She was clever, of course," says Max. "Damnably clever. No one would guess meeting her that she was not the kindest, most generous, most gifted person in the world" (20). But Rebecca is at the very least a somewhat unknowable character, assessed entirely through hearsay: du Maurier herself commented that she "was certainly an enigma and intended to be such". Initially, argues Alison Light, she is

> a figment of the [narrator's] imagination, invented from a sense of her own social and sexual limitations. 'Rebecca' is a projection of her own desires which both help to produce and ratify the girl's feelings of inadequacy.

She becomes an embodiment of "Beauty, brains and breeding" (20), an icon of femininity, beside which the narrator is always deficient. Thereafter, she suddenly becomes the opposite. And throughout there is enough ambiguity to sustain many different readings.

Certainly, readers have often admired her. "Long after the book has been closed, which character reverberates in the memory?" asks Sally Beauman. "Rebecca." She has frequently been seen as feminist rebel – an attractive character because she represents freedom from society's gender-based expectations. "She did what she liked, she lived as she liked," according to Mrs Danvers: she had the "courage and spirit of a boy" (18).

It is worth noting that she behaves exactly like many upper-class men of the period. She cuts her hair short, rides horses fast, sails alone, and has affairs in London – while outwardly respecting the moral standards of the period (on the precipice at Monte Carlo, she makes a "bargain" with Max to "look after your precious Manderley", and make people "say we are the luckiest, happiest, handsomest couple in all England" [20]). It is implied that she is sexually insatiable. The satyr, a figure of unbridled sexuality, is visible from her study window. Later, we learn that she had a number of lovers; Max compares her to an "animal" in her "degradation" (20).

John Sutherland suggests that she has "lesbian credentials". This may be another exaggeration. But Mrs Danvers, who seems very preoccupied with her bed and clothes, says that she "despised all men. She was above all that" (24); while Maxim says, somewhat vaguely, that she was "not even normal" (20). We learn that she is unable to fulfil the traditional female role by having children, due to a "malformation of the uterus" (26). Her ultimate sin, suggests Beauman, is "undermining the entire patriarchal edifice that is Manderley". Is that, perhaps, why she had to die?

Mrs Danvers

Mrs Danvers is a classic bogeywoman, often invoked and parodied by other writers. She has been called a haunted house in human form: du Maurier used her "in lieu of the hauntings of gothic melodrama", suggests Veronica Horwell. When she first appears, on the narrator's arrival at Manderley, she is linked immediately with death:

> *Someone advanced from the sea of faces, someone tall and gaunt, dressed in deep black, whose prominent cheek-bones and great, hollow eyes gave her a skull's face, parchment-white, set on a skeleton's frame. (7)*

Her hand is "limp and heavy, deathly cold"; and her "skull's face" in mentioned repeatedly later on in the book. She is a kind of emissary of the dead: she stands in for Rebecca, furious that the second Mrs de Winter is trying to take her place.

Initially, Mrs Danvers acts as the gatekeeper to an alien and intimidating world, and seems unimpressed by her humble new mistress. But gradually the narrator realises that there is something beside scorn and snobbery "in those eyes of hers, something surely of positive dislike, or actual malice?" (7). Mrs Danvers persecutes her new mistress, and does it in a particularly creepy way: she haunts her, "a black figure" at the head of the stairs (7); she appears at windows, and suddenly materialises behind the narrator in Rebecca's empty bedroom in the disused wing.

As the book proceeds, her behaviour becomes ever more extreme and manipulative. She is furious that the narrator has "tried to take Mrs de Winter's place" (18). She seems to feed off the narrator's unhappiness and feelings of inferiority, which leave her "triumphant, gloating, excited in a strangely unhealthy way" (14). She convinces the narrator to dress up as Caroline de Winter, in a "cruel and evil" (18) attempt to worsen an already shaky marriage. When the narrator confronts her afterwards, Mrs Danvers tries to get her employer's wife to commit suicide.

Mrs Danvers is clearly fixated with her dead mistress. "She simply adored Rebecca," Beatrice tells the narrator (9). In the scene in Rebecca's bedroom, in Chapter 14, we get some sense of the extent of her obsession. We learn that Mrs Danvers comes to the room every day and dusts it, as if it were a shrine to the dead. There seem to be sexual undertones to her fixation: she praises her mistress's "beautiful figure", touches her clothes lovingly, and boasts that Rebecca wouldn't allow anyone else to brush her hair. Mrs Danvers has often been seen as a lesbian; Hitchcock's film, in which she was memorably played by Judith Anderson, emphasised this angle (though it's worth remembering that Anderson's version is probably 20 years younger than du Maurier's, who looked after Rebecca from childhood). Certainly, she seems jealous and possessive. When she learns that Rebecca concealed her illness from her, she says: "Why did she keep it from me? She told me everything" (25). At the end of the film, she disappears shortly after Favell makes a telephone call. It is implied that she starts the fire at Manderley – her final act as Rebecca's agent.

Symbols and images

Manderley

Some people would argue that in *Rebecca* the house is a fully-fledged character rather than a mere symbol: at various points it is said to be "alive", and it looms over much of the story (16). Alfred Hitchcock said that of the four main presences in the book – Maxim, his two wives, and the house – the house was the dominant one. It looms, of course, from the very first line – before we even identify any of the characters – to the final paragraph, and provides both the setting for the action and the focus for many of the novel's themes. Manderley appears in the first chapter at the centre of a disturbing dream, where it has a variety of different qualities: initially enigmatic, impassive and beautiful ("secretive and silent", with "perfect symmetry"); then briefly redolent of domestic happiness; then a symbol of painful, irrecoverable loss (a "desolate shell"). It also conceals a painful secret ("...our fear and suffering lay buried in the ruins.").

According to Freud, the house in dreams is often a symbol of "the human person as a whole", with cellars and attics representing repressed desires and guilty secrets. In everyday language, and particularly in Gothic stories, a house often stands for a family and its fates. Manderley is what psychoanalysts would call an "overdetermined" symbol, suggesting multiple wishes and fears in one image.

Similarly, in the novel at large Manderly stands for a wide variety of notions. Early on in the story, it means aristocratic splendour: Mrs Van Hopper introduces Maxim as "the man who owns Manderley" (2) later adding that this "lovely

Opposite: One of the posters for Alfred Hitchcock's Academy Award-winning film adaptation of Rebecca

Selznick International PRESENTS

Rebecca

with

Laurence OLIVIER . Joan FONTAINE

DIRECTED BY
ALFRED HITCHCOCK
From
DAVID O. SELZNICK
Producer of
GONE WITH THE WIND
Based On the Novel by
DAPHNE DU MAURIER
Released thru UNITED ARTISTS

home" has been "in his family's possession since the conquest" (3). Its grandness casts a powerful spell on those around him. When Maxim asks why Mrs Van Hopper considers him of importance, the narrator replies: "Because of Manderley" (4).

The narrator has a deep feeling for the house, too, rooted partly in childhood when she bought a postcard of it. Yet she notes that Maxim seems both proud and wary on the subject. "Maybe there was something about Manderley that made it a place apart; it would not bear discussion" (4). When the narrator finally visits, it is initially menacing. The drive "twisted and turned like a serpent", passing through "dark and silent woods", then "shocking" rhododendrons and between "blood-red walls". It is of course beautiful and enviable, living up to its reputation:"A thing of grace, exquisite and faultless, lovelier even than I had ever dreamed..."(7). But it proves - as the omens have suggested – to be a very ambiguous possession.

From the narrator's point of view, Manderley embodies the presence of Rebecca, the threatening and superior other woman. As we have seen, everything about the house and its running reminds the narrator of her predecessor. Indeed Rebecca seems actually to haunt it; it is suggested at various points that "she was in the house still", that "Rebecca was still mistress of Manderley" (18). Only after the catharsis of the discovery that Maxim hated Rebecca does the narrator assert ownership:

Standing there, looking down upon it from the banks, I realized, perhaps for the first time, with a funny feeling of bewilderment and pride that it was my home, I belonged there, and Manderley belonged to me. (19)

Even then, her ownership is only temporary: Rebecca is expelled, but she seems to take the house with her.

By contrast, feminist critics have pointed out that Manderley also embodies the patriarchal system: hierarchical, claustrophobic and oppressive for the women who live in it. The word "man" features prominently in the name itself (and Maxim is "the man who owns Manderley"); it is the scene of the narrator's awkward and painful attempts to mould herself into a correct and pleasing feminine role. It is also true that Maxim seems to be compelled towards onerous forms of correctness by the house. He keeps up a sham marriage with the unfaithful Rebecca which disgusts him, primarily out of respect for the house and his position. "I put Manderley first, before everything else... I accepted everything, because of Manderley" (20). And indeed the final straw which compels him to kill Rebecca is her taunt to him that her illegitimate child will inherit his house and lands:

"It would grow up here in Manderley, bearing your name... It would give you the biggest thrill of your life, wouldn't it, Max, to watch my son grow bigger day by day, and to know that when you died, all this would be his?" (20)

The sea

The sea plays an important role in the novel; and it is often linked to Rebecca. She is frequently mentioned in connection with the sea or water, from the first mention of her having drowned in the bay. When the narrator arrives at the house, she and Maxim are given the less grand rooms in the east wing, facing the rose garden – which is domesticated and confined. By contrast, what Mrs Danvers calls "Mrs de Winter's bedroom" – the "big room" – looks "down to the sea" (7). It is revealed that Rebecca loved sailing and set up the cottage in the bay as a retreat away from Maxim and Manderley. Like her, the sea is wild and untamed. Water is also traditionally associated with powerful and disturbing forms of femininity: witches were said never to sink or drown.

The narrator's unease about her new life focuses specifically on the sea. The "dull, persistent sound" of the waves plays "a jagged tune upon the nerves" (11). It becomes, like Rebecca, a kind of taboo subject. She begins "to dread any mention of the sea, for the sea might lead to boats, to accidents, to drowning..." She twice says that she is glad to be facing inland: "I preferred the rose garden, after all, to the sound of the sea" (9). On the occasions when she ventures into Rebecca's bedroom, or is otherwise particularly aware of her lingering presence, the sea is always mentioned. "I could hear the sound of the sea very plainly" (14). "The sound of the sea came to me through the open window, the soft hissing sound of the ebb-tide leaving the shingle" (17). When Mrs Danvers appears and tells the (supposed) story of Rebecca's death, she says: "You know now... why Mr de Winter does not use these rooms any more. Listen to the sea" (14).

As the tension mounts, the narrator's agitation is again explicitly linked to the sea in various ways, both literal and symbolic. A sea mist appears, causing the accident that will lead to Rebecca's discovery and heralding her return. It also becomes an image of the hidden and repressed past which will inevitably resurface:

I knew now the reason for my sense of foreboding. It was not the stranded ship that was sinister, nor the crying gulls, nor the thin black funnel pointing to the shore. It was the stillness of the black water, and the unknown things that lay beneath. It was the diver going down to those cool quiet depths and stumbling upon Rebecca's boat, and Rebecca's dead companion. (19)

In the aftermath, the narrator finds herself repeating the words "Time and Tide wait for for no man" in her head (20). In the wake of Rebecca's reappearance, it rains steadily – just as, in Maxim's account, it rains after Rebecca's body has been sunk in the bay. A final invocation of the sea comes in the novel's last sentence, even its last word: "And the ashes blew towards us with the salt wind from the sea" (27).

Ghosts

Another word for a ghost is a revenant – a person who returns from the dead. This is a usage explicitly pointed to by the "queer prophetic name" of Rebecca's boat, *Je Reviens* (21). Rebecca is full of invocations of ghosts and hauntings, and the idea of coming or going back. In the first chapter, the narrator imagines that a "nervous poacher" trespassing on the ruins Manderley might hear a ghostly figure of "a woman in evening dress". Even in Monte Carlo, the narrator says, "I was following a phantom in my mind" (5). On discovering the dedication from Rebecca to Max in the book of poems, the narrator describes the her as "dead", but her writing as "alive" (6).

At Manderley, Rebecca manifests herself in the narrator's mind as a supernatural presence – very much as in a ghost story. Sitting in the first Mrs de

Winter's chair: "Unconsciously I shivered as though someone had opened the door behind me and let a draught into the room" (7). Seated at her desk, the narrator thinks: "At any moment she might come back into the room and she would see me there..." (8). Rebecca's cottage down at the shore makes her "a little fearful": she thinks that there might be something "horrible" there (10). She describes herself as waiting for "the return of the hostess" (11).

Gradually, all this builds up to the scene in the deserted wing of the house – again, a classic ghost story trope – where Rebecca's presence asserts itself in all sorts of ways: in her clothes, her scent, creating a "growing sense of horror" in the narrator (14). Turning around – again, as in a ghost story – she sees Mrs Danvers, who reveals that "I feel her everywhere. You do too, don't you?" She asks the narrator: "Do you think the dead can come back and haunt the living?" This, ultimately, is exactly what Rebecca does. "Her body had come back," says the narrator after the boat is found (21). The idea of coming back features in various other contexts. After visiting the cottage in the bay, the narrator berates herself for opening up "a road into the past again" – while Maxim declares: "Oh, God, what a fool I was to come back" (11). Thanks to Mrs Danvers's machinations, the narrator herself acts out the return of the first Mrs de Winter, by wearing her fancy dress outfit: Maxim's face is "ashen white", as if he had seen a ghost.

Freud said that we are unable to comprehend death, that "no human being really grasps it". Thoughts of death, perpetually repressed, are thus reworked into projections of hope or fear, particularly where guilt and violent death are involved – manifesting themselves as fantasies of contact with the departed, or nightmarish visions of the returning dead. The story of *Rebecca* acts out the return of these repressed events: of Maxim's secrets, and of the narrator's fears.

Doubling and mirroring

As Sally Beauman points out, du Maurier's work is full of "splitting, doubling and mirroring devices ". Her novel *The Scapegoat* (1957) , for instance, features two men who are so similar-looking that one can inhabit the other's life. And in *Rebecca*, as we have seen, the narrator and the first Mrs de Winter are constantly set up in binary opposition. They almost seem to be mirror images of each other: where Rebecca is supremely confident, runs Manderley with flair and competence, and can sail and ride horses, the narrator is the opposite. They both share one identity – that of Mrs de Winter – which serves to underline their differences. When the narrator and Beatrice visit Maxim's grandmother, the old lady is befuddled and distressed. "Bee, who is this child?" she asks. "Why did you not bring Rebecca? Where is dear Rebecca?" (15). Equally, Ben tells her that she is "not like the other one" (13). Such is the narrator's sense of inadequacy that when someone calls to ask for Mrs de Winter, she replies: "I'm afraid you have made a mistake... Mrs de Winter has been dead for a year" (8). Later, shortly before she comes close to convincing the narrator to commit suicide, Mrs de Winter declares that Rebecca is "the real Mrs de Winter, not you" (18).

The are several additional doubling figures in the novel: for instance, the east wing and the west wing, the sea and the rose garden. There are even two paths in the woods, one leading to Happy Valley, which is soothing and full of beautiful flowers, and on to a pleasant cove; the other leading through a dark unpleasant wood with a tree that looks like "the white bleached limb of a skeleton", which leads to "the other beach" – the site of Rebecca's cottage and her murder (10). Furthermore, Maxim's grandmother has "a strong, uncanny resemblance to her grandson" (15).

Conversely, there are also various instances where the narrator seems to merge her own identity with Rebecca's. Thinking herself into her predecessor's position at dinner, she finds that "I had so identified myself with Rebecca that my own dull self did not exist" (16). Maxim is disturbed; he says that she looks "like a common criminal".

Then, before the fancy dress ball, she delights in her transformation into Caroline de Winter: "I don't think I have ever felt so excited before, so happy and so proud" (16).

At this point she does not, of course, realise that she has also transformed herself into Rebecca, but she seems to enjoy her transformation. Looking at herself in the mirror, she "did not recognise the face that stared at me in the glass. The eyes were larger surely, the mouth narrower, the skin white and clear?" Others form the same impression. "Identical," says Maxim. "The same picture, the same dress. You stood there on the stairs, and for one ghastly moment I thought..." (17).

Later on, when she is more confident of Maxim's love and thus her identity, the narrator tells Mrs Danvers: "I am Mrs de Winter now, you know" (21). But there is an uneasy sense that Rebecca may have possessed her, or infiltrated her personality. The narrator dreams, while en route to Manderley after Maxim has been cleared, that her writing starts to resemble Rebecca's. She goes to the mirror:

> *A face stared back at me that was not my own. It was very pale, very lovely, framed in a cloud of dark hair. The eyes narrowed and smiled. The lips parted. The face in the glass stared back at me and laughed. (27)*

The figure of the double is doing complex work in

the novel: pointing up oppositions and jealousies, registering the narrator's ongoing crisis of identity, and lending an uncanny atmosphere to the whole story. Du Maurier said of *The Scapegoat* that it was her own story , and that of her husband – who were both mentally unbalanced at the time. "We are both doubles. So it is with everyone. Every one of us has his, or her, dark side. Which is to overcome the other? This is the purpose of the book. And it ends, as you know, with the problem unsolved..."

Fires and forbidden books

Rebecca is rich in symbols, and there are many others that feature in the novel. For instance, Rebecca is often linked to the colour red: "blood-red" rhododendrons (7); red roses; the sky "shot with crimson, like a splash of blood" at the end of the book (27); and of course, the blood that seeps onto the cottage floor when Maxim shoots her.

Another recurring symbol is that of the forbidden book. When talking to Maxim in Monaco about a dressmaker's attempt to bribe her, the narrator is "aware of that sick, unhealthy feeling I had experienced as a child when turning the pages of a forbidden book" (4). Later on, when Mrs Danvers is trying to encourage her to visit Rebecca's room, the image recurs. The housekeeper's insistence reminds her "of a visit to a friend's house, as a child, when the daughter of the house, older than me, took my arm and whispered in my ear, 'I know where there is a book, locked in a cupboard, in my mother's bedroom. Shall we go and look at it?" (9).

Later still, after the narrator has disturbed Maxim by imagining herself in Rebecca's place, her husband complains that her face has changed. When asked to explain, he inquires whether, when she was young, she was "ever forbidden to read certain books, and did your father put these books under lock and key?" (16). When she replies in the affirmative, he says: "A husband is not so very different from a father after all. There is a certain type of knowledge I prefer you not to have."

It's an odd metaphor, the meaning of which is not entirely apparent. But it seems to have a sexual connotation: a forbidden book which a Victorian father might hide; something to do with "knowledge". The narrator is very innocent at the beginning of the story: when Frank says that the narrator, if not as beautiful as Rebecca, has other qualities which a husband might value more – kindness, sincerity and "modesty", she doesn't know quite what to think. She had imagined that modesty was "something to do with with minding meeting people in a passage on the way to the bathroom" (11). Of course it becomes clear what he means when she learns more about Rebecca. The idea of secret knowledge being locked up could be seen as a reference to the Bluebeard myth:

the disturbing truths that the young wife discovers about her husband; the locked room, like Rebecca's, where evidence of the previous wives' fates is concealed. When reading the book of poems signed by Rebecca, the narrator feels "rather like someone peering through the keyhole of locked door" (4); while the "sensual and horrible" (4) Favell tells Maxim to "make the most of your night behind the locked door," (25) on the night before the trip to London.

There are certainly other half-submerged sexual images in the book. As Maxim drives up to Manderley for the first time, there are frequent suggestive words and phrases: "penetrate", "throbbing", "penetrating ever deeper" (7). The narrator drops and breaks a figure of Cupid, the god of erotic love. Visible from the window at Rebecca's desk is a satyr playing his pipes (18). In classical mythology, the satyr, half-goat, is a figure of sexual excess. When they read the press coverage about the discovery of Rebecca's boat, the narrator remarks that Maxim, with his "young bride" is made to sound "vile... a sort of satyr" (22): again, a bit like Bluebeard.

Interpretations

Oedipus and Electra

It is often said that *Rebecca* feels like a myth or a fairy-tale. As mentioned, it has been compared to the stories of Cinderella and Bluebeard. Sally Beauman calls it "part Grimm's fairytale, part Freudian family romance"; she, among other critics, remarks on the story's strong Oepidal undertones. In Freud, the Oedipus complex describes the child's desire (whether overt or unconscious) to have sexual relations with the parent of the opposite sex, and displace or even kill the parent of the same sex. The term refers to the mythical king of Thebes, who unwittingly killed his father and married his mother. (In women, it is sometimes called the Electra complex – a phrase coined by Carl Jung, whose work du Maurier knew.)

Richard Kelly suggests that du Maurier fused the methods of psychological realism with an Oepidal version of the Cinderella story:

The nameless heroine has been saved from a life of drudgery by marrying a handsome, wealthy aristocrat, but unlike the Prince in *Cinderella*, Maxim de Winter is old enough to be the narrator's father. The narrator thus must do battle with The Other Woman – the dead Rebecca and her witch-like surrogate, Mrs

Danvers – to win the love of her husband and father-figure. The fantasy of this novel is fulfilled when Maxim confesses to the narrator that he never loved Rebecca; indeed, he hated her, a confession that allows the narrator to emerge triumphantly from the Oedipal triangle.

This, Kelly suggests, is part of the explanation for the book's enduring appeal:

> Millions have identified with the plain, nameless narrator of *Rebecca*, a woman who defines her personality by overcoming the mother-figure of Rebecca to win the lasting love of her father-lover.

Though it may sound outlandish, there is in fact a great deal of evidence in the text to support this thesis. Maxim frequently refers to the narrator as a daughter or a child. "I suppose you are young enough to be my daughter, and I don't know how to deal with you," he tells her during their courtship (5). He calls her "my sweet child" (11); she complains that he treats her "as a child" (16); his grandmother asks, "Who is this child?" (15). Maxim tells the narrator that "A husband is not so very different from a father after all" (16). Mrs Danvers complains that she is "young enough to be his daughter" – yet she is trying "to take Mrs de Winter's place" (18).

The resolution of the story comes when she

does successfully take Rebecca's place in Maxim's affections. After learning that he never loved Rebecca, and killed her, we are told that it was "as though I had entered into a new phase of my life and nothing would be quite the same" (19). "I've grown up, Maxim, in 24 hours," she tells him. "I'll never be a child again." Where before their marriage had been loveless and sterile, it now seems to be passionately sexual: "He had not kissed me like this before." And finally, he says "I love you" (20). Later, they "kiss one another, feverishly, desperately, like guilty lovers who have not kissed before" (25). The narrator describes her success, furthermore, as a kind of murder: "I too had killed Rebecca, I too had sunk the boat there in the bay" (20).

It is worth remarking, too, that Oedipal relationships are a running theme in du Maurier's books . Father-daughter incest features in her early novel *The Progress of Julius* (1933), and in the short story 'The Borderline Case'. Her novel *My Cousin Rachel* (1951), perhaps the best of her post-war career, is another Oedipal tale: it is a kind of mirror image of *Rebecca,* in which the young man becomes obsessed with his adopted father's wife. Though it is not strictly relevant to the textual analysis of her novels, these stories may be echoes of du Maurier's own life: she felt her mother Muriel was cold and distant, and she was very close to her father, the actor-manager George du Maurier, who was violently and inappropriately jealous of the young men in her life.

Rebecca and feminism

In their influential critical study *The Madwoman in the Attic,* Sandra Gilbert and Susan Guba pointed out that the patriarchal norms of 19th century Britain tended to cast women as either the "angel" or the "monster" – and that the more interesting women authors of the period adopted these norms in their writing, but in an often subversive and warped fashion. They argued that, running through 19th century women's novels and poetry, were out-of-control female characters, "maddened doubles" who "functioned as asocial surrogates" for their more "docile" female characters. The most famous example gave Gilbert and Gubar's book its title: Bertha Rochester, imprisoned in her husband's attic, bearing witness to the confined, subordinate role of women and the forbidden anger of Charlotte Brontë's well-behaved heroine, Jane Eyre.

Du Maurier, as we have seen, was deeply influenced by 19th century fiction, and particularly by *Jane Eyre.* In *Rebecca* she recycled Brontë's doubling device, which contrasts the bad first wife with the good second wife; and she created something even more warped and subversive out of the pairing. On the face of it, the novel submits entirely to the dominant patriarchal norms of its time. The story is about the taming of a powerful woman, a "monster" who asserts her sexual freedom and defies the traditional male-dominated order. Rebecca, as we have seen, behaves like a roguish man of the era; she is unfaithful and an open threat to male primogeniture. The book duly punishes her: she is killed, expunged from Manderley – and all evidence of her murder is erased.

As Alison Light suggests, romance fiction can be seen as a "coercive and stereotyping" form: it invites the reader "to identify with a passive heroine who only finds true happiness in submitting to a masterful male". Yet, she argues, *Rebecca* provides a "classic model of romance fiction while at the same time exposing some of its terms". That is, perhaps, an understatement. It is a Cinderella story that becomes a Bluebeard story – where the marriage, instead of being a happily-ever-after sort of place, turns out to be a crime scene. The hero is a murderer and the heroine becomes his accomplice; its female villain is in some ways the most attractive and memorable character. As Sally Beauman writes, "thanks to the cunning of du Maurier's narrative structure, [readers] were able to condemn Rebecca (a promiscuous woman – what other option did they have?); but secretly respond to the anger, rebellion and vengefulness she embodies".

Du Maurier's fiction is preoccupied with the balance of power in marriage. Her early books, says Helen Taylor, examine "unreliable and ruthless male desire"; the sacrifice of women by men is a recurring theme throughout her career. *Rebecca* uses the Gothic novel – a traditionally feminine form, and a way of exploring female fear of powerful fathers and violent husbands – to examine the position of women. The narrator, dependent on strangers for her keep, is passed from father to husband without even being given her own name. Manderley – a bastion of patriarchy – is confining and paralysing.

Harking back, again, to the Bluebeard theme, the narrator describes herself when she arrives there as a sacrificial victim, remembering "a sea of faces, open-mouthed and curious, gazing at me as though they were the watching crowd about the block, and I the victim with my hands behind my back" (7). Her husband, as we have seen, is an overbearing and sinister figure, linked in various ways with violence. The narrator finds herself constantly held up to a spirit-crushing ideal of feminine behaviour, personified in the form of her ghostly predecessor. In the end, her position is supposedly resolved; yet it is an uneasy and pyrrhic victory. In this area, as in so many other areas, *Rebecca* is a deeply ambivalent novel. Du Maurier both satisfies and undermines our conventional expectations as readers. The novel's "circular structure", suggests Light, "tries to mop up and gloss over the disorder at its centre". But questions are always left hanging in the air.

How good is *Rebecca*?

Rebecca has been dismissed as a serious work of art many times. In the past, as we have seen, du Maurier was often categorised as a "Romantic novelist", an author of derivative "novelettes" for women readers of limited intelligence. At the time of publication, V.S. Pritchett was fairly typical in regarding it as a rattling good yarn, but nothing more. In his review, he conceded that "many a better novelist would give his eyes to be able to tell a story as Miss du Maurier does, to make it move at such a pace and to go with such mastery from surprise to surprise". He added that anyone "who starts this book will not be able to put it down until he has finished it; after that, I hope that he will wake up and laugh at himself". Certainly, *Rebecca* has attracted plenty of derision over the years: it teeters on the edge of absurdity, which is why it has so often been parodied.

More recently, Patricia Beer suggested that while du Maurier was "a great storyteller", she "can hardly be convincingly presented as a great novelist". Beer quotes E.M. Forster, who called storytelling a "low atavistic form" – very different from the higher art of fiction. The novel, she maintains, "has more to give than just a story... du Maurier's novels, it seems to me, do not."

Even *Rebecca*'s greatest admirers acknowledge that the novel has serious weaknesses. Some aspects have dated badly, such as the "half-wit" Ben. Sally Beauman calls it "melodramatic in places"; she singles out Maxim's confession, told in dialogue form, as a little "hollow". Du Maurier's dialogue, in particular, can be weak. Mrs Danvers's long romantic speeches are clearly overwrought, while Jack Favell's exclamations verge on the silly:

> *"Drunk, am I?' shouted Favell. "Oh, no, my fine friend. You may be a magistrate and a colonel into the bargain, but it won't cut any ice with me." (24).*

Or:

> *"You crazy little rat," said Favell slowly, "you bloody crazy little rat."*

Overall, it is the quality of her prose that is most often criticised. "One barrier, I think, to du Maurier's recognition as a serious writer has been her indifference to the raw material of language," argues Lorna Scott Fox, complaining that "her technique was unliterary". As we have seen in the section about the novel's style, du Maurier's writing is arguably excessive, repetitive and crude at times; her own editor said that she simply wasn't "interested" in the minor details. Her writing, suggests Patricia Beer, was "undistinguished at best and cack-handed at worst".

On the other hand, many have argued that her sometimes undistinguished prose does not stop her fiction from being interesting and powerful. As the novelist Sarah Waters put it,

> du Maurier's writing is a bit ropey at times, but her novels and stories are fantastically moody and resonant, and *Rebecca*, in particular, just feels so fundamentally right – like a myth, or a fairy tale.

Lorna Scott Fox agrees, suggesting that in fact the very lack of sophistication gives her work power: "the clarity of the first-person voice makes us feel at one with the narrator's madness: we are possessed by every changing mood, hypnotised by the fantastic delirium of events." Slavok Zizek takes the point even further, arguing that du Maurier's artlessness allows her a kind of direct access to our fantasy lives:

> Her prose seems marked by a melodramatic excess that often comes dangerously close to the ridiculous – after reading one of her books, it is

difficult to avoid the vague sentiment that it is no longer possible to write like that today. She writes without truly being a writer; in what then, resides the secret of the undisputed tremendous power of fascination exerted by her stories? What if these two features are somehow connected? What if her lack of style, her pathetic directness, is the formal effect of the fact that du Maurier's narratives directly, all too directly, stage the fantasies that sustain our lives?

Clearly *Rebecca*'s real fascination lies in its psychological depths and its symbolic resonance , rather than its fine literary style (though her writing, as we have seen, is very effective at creating atmosphere).

The power of the novel, argues Sally Beauman, comes from "its imagery, symmetry, poetry, mythic resonance and psychological truth". But equally, it is possible that not enough credit is given to du Maurier for the skill that imparts those qualities to *Rebecca* – that gives it what Sarah Waters calls its rightness. To take one example, I hope this guide shows how carefully and coherently the book's symbols are developed, and how they interlock closely with both its themes and its characters. Manderley, for instance, symbolises the class system, and the narrator's jealousy, and Maxim's troubled past. The often-reiterated theme of "going back" to the past, meanwhile, is symbolised by the ghostly figures that haunt the text, and enacted by the novel's circular structure; the idea of time is linked, in the repeated phrase "Time and Tide wait for no man" (20), to the idea of the sea – and thus, literally, to the idea of Rebecca's body being discovered. Furthermore, du Maurier shows a very impressive ability to construct a gripping, cohesive and satisfying narrative which is nevertheless deeply ambivalent at almost every level: one that has been interpreted as both snobbish and deeply critical of the class system; both fiercely feminist and reactionary in its sexual politics.

Helen Taylor argues that du Maurier deserves to be taken seriously as a "complex writer", pointing out that much recent criticism has identified in her work rich, challenging themes "of incestuous desire, doppelganger figures, dynastic and dysfunctional families, polymorphous or multiple sexualities, and fractured notions of appropriate class and gender roles, as well as drawing attention to her literary experimentation with narrative voices and inconclusive endings". This, she suggests, has "helped transform a writer pigeon-holed as romantic and parochially regional into a significant literary figure ". According to Richard Kelly, *Rebecca* in particular "is a profound and fascinating study of an obsessive personality, of sexual dominance, of human identity and of the liberation of the hidden self".

Plenty would still disagree with this assessment, and would argue that there is simply too much formulaic plotting, bad prose, and contrivance in du Maurier's work to justify treating her as a great writer. At best, they would say that she was on the borderline between popular fiction and real art; at worst, perhaps, best appreciated as enjoyable kitsch. The film critic Pauline Kael, for instance, admired the film *Rebecca* – which has a lighter and more campy tone than the book – but only as "magnificent Gothic romantic corn". Either way, *R ebecca* is likely to endure, outlasting both its admirers and its detractors.

A SHORT CHRONOLOGY

1847 Charlotte Brontë's *Jane Eyre.*

1907 May 13 Daphne du Maurier is born.

1931 *The Loving Spirit,* du Maurier's first novel.

1932 du Maurier marries Lieutenant-Colonel Frederick "Tommy" Browning in Cornwall.

1936 *Jamaica Inn.*

1938 *Rebecca.*

1940 Oscar winning film adaptation of *Rebecca* directed by Alfred Hitchcock is released.

1951 *My Cousin Rachel.*

1963 Alfred Hitchcock's film of *The Birds,* based on a novellete by du Maurier.

1969 Du Maurier is made a Dame in the Queen's birthday honours list.

1993 June 19 du Maurier dies at Kilmarth.

1997 Jim O'Brien's television adaptation of *Rebecca.*

FURTHER READING

Daphne du Maurier - *The Rebecca Notebook* (Virago , 2004)

Margaret Forster - *Daphne du Maurier* (Arrow , 1994)

Sandra Gilbert & Susan Gubar - *The Madwoman in the Attic* (Yale, 1979)

Richard Kelly - *Daphne du Maurier* (Twayne, 1987)

Tania Modleski - *Loving with a Vengeance* (Routledge, 2008) Contains the article "The Female Uncanny: Gothic Novels for Women"

Patsy Stoneman - *Brontë Transformations* (Harvester Wheatsheaf, 1996)

John Sutherland - *Where Was Rebecca Shot?* (Phoenix , 1999)

Maria Tatar - *Secrets Beyond the Door* (Princeton, 2006) Contains the article "Daphne du Maurier's Rebecca and Modern Gothics"

Helen Taylor, ed. - *The Daphne du Maurier Companion* (Virago, 2007) Contains, among other articles: Christopher Frayling - "Preface"; Helen Taylor - "Introduction"; Sheila Hodges - "Editing Daphne du Maurier"; Rebecca

Munford - "Spectres of Authorship: Daphne du Maurier's Gothic Legacy"; Sally Beauman - "Rebecca" - also featured as the afterword to the Virago edition of Rebecca Antonia Fraser; "Rebecca's Story", with an epilogue by du Maurier

Patricia Beer - "Something about her eyes" *London Review of Books* 24 June 1993

Veronica Horwell - "Mrs Danvers, a manipulatively spiteful bogeywoman" *The Guardian*, 31 October 2014

Christian House - "Daphne du Maurier always said her novel Rebecca was a study in jealousy" *Daily Telegraph*, 17 Aug 2013

Pauline Kael - "Rebecca"

Richard Kelly - Obituary *The Independent* 21 April 1989

Alison Light - "Returning to Manderley - Romance Fiction, Female Sexuality and Class" *Feminist Review 16* (1984)

Joanna Russ - "Someone's Trying to Kill Me and I think it's my husband: The Modern Gothic." *The Journal of Popular Culture*, Volume 6, Issue 4, pages 666–691, Spring 1973

Lorna Scott Fox - "More Fun to Be a Boy" *London Review of Books* 2 November 2000

Slavoj Zizek - "Are We Allowed to Enjoy Daphne du Maurier?"

Notes

First published in 2016 by
Connell Guides
Artist House
35 Little Russell Street
London WC1A 2HH

10 9 8 7 6 5 4 3 2 1

Picture credits:

p.21 © REX Features
p.53 © REX Features

A CIP catalogue record for this book is available from the British Library.
ISBN 978-1-907776-93-9

Design © Nathan Burton
Written by Theo Tait
Edited by Jolyon Connell

Assistant Editors and typeset by
Paul Woodward and Holly Bruce

www.connellguides.com

Printed and bound by CPI Group (UK) Ltd, Croydon, CR0 4YY